POWER

OF

WORDS

30 WORDS THAT CAN MAKE OR BREAK YOUR MINDSET, SELF-ESTEEM, AND SELF-WORTH

DEDICATION

To Jon, my family, and to those who always told me to
GO FOR IT!

Thank you and I love you.

TABLE OF CONTENTS

Part B: Power Words...Error! Bookmark not defined.

INTRODUCTION

Sticks and stones may break your bones, but words will never hurt me.

Ever heard those words before?

Yea, so have I.

How much truth does that hold, though?

WORDS ARE POWER and they can either make you or break you! But how you use those words is how it will affect you now and for the rest of your life.

It all started on a normal day sitting in my 5th-grade science class with desks all gathered together in small groups. Looking around the classroom, all the girls were grouped and all the boys were grouped, preparing to work on a science project, except me. An awkward little girl sitting with all boys, I pulled my chair back, confused on why I was not with all the other girls. I confronted my teacher and asked her if I could please sit with the rest of the girls in the class. To my surprise, my teacher blatantly tells me to my face, "Te vas a sentar con todos los burros, porque tu eres una burra." Let me translate that for you, "you are a very smart young lady, so you will sit with all the smart kids!"

Yea, that is not what she said…

"You will sit with all of the dumb kids, because that is who you are, DUMB!"

Now, I don't know about you, but that is one crazy thing to say to a 10-year-old little girl in front of the entire class.

That day was the beginning of my story of how I let that WORD "DUMB" become a representation of who I was until now.

As I carried that word with me through middle school and into high school, I let that word take over me, and I received a reminder of that when I entered High School in my English 1 Pre-AP Class.

I struggled in school, I was not your top student, but I was your average student in school. Good grades participated in extracurricular activities and overall did well in school.

However, I got a second dose of the word DUMB when my English 1 Teacher pulled me out of class to talk about how I was not smart enough to be in her classroom and should change my class schedule.

Now, this was not 10-year-old little me anymore. But, the WORD still held power over me, but this time I let it challenge me. I stayed in the class, I struggled, but I made it through!

Sticks and stones may break your bones, but words will never hurt me.

I guess you can say it holds some truth to it as long as you believe it.

The next 20 words I will share with you is to show you how a word can easily make you feel broken and can challenge your self-worth, self-esteem and overall your mindset and how you view yourself and life.

As we go through the first 10 BREAK WORDS, I want you to think of any situations you have been in and go down memory lane to challenge these words and then use them to MAKE YOU a better person and create a positive MINDSET, SELF-WORTH, and SEL-ESTEEM.

This was such a challenge for me as I went down memory lane and therefore, I hope this book will help you as much as it helped me.

BROKEN WORDS

STICKS AND
STONES MAY
BREAK MY BONES
BUT
WORDS WILL
NEVER HURT ME

CHAPTER 1

DUMB

Where did the word DUMB come from? And how have we allowed it to become such a powerful word we connect it with feeling we are not smart enough, that we allow it to knock us down and feel we can't ever reach the top?

Did you know that according to the dictionary, the word DUMB is defined as someone unwilling to speak and has no connection to our intelligence? People have been using the word DUMB incorrectly, who would have thought?

Think back to a time or a person that has ever called you DUMB!

(I want you to grab a piece of paper and write down what came to your mind- quick note)

How did it make you feel?

What happened or why did that person feel it was ok to call you that?

How long have you held on to that word in your life?

(Rip the paper into shreds, toss it away in the trash, let this be the last time you think of this person and how it made you feel. You are free from this broken word.)

CHAPTER 2

STUPID

Such a common word we use loosely, we hear it on TV, we hear it at school, and we hear it at home. That we hear it so often, that we associate that word with something that is not worthy and a stab at our level of intelligence.

Even though people connect the word DUMB and STUPID as having the same meaning, remember if you go back to *#1, DUMB* has no association with our intelligence, but the word STUPID holds that power.

If I got paid a $1 for every time someone called me stupid because they felt I could never be smarter than them, I was not smart enough to go to college. I was stupid for just being me. I would probably be a millionaire.

Can you think of a time you called someone stupid or maybe someone has called you that?

How did that make you feel? And how do you think that made the person feel as well?

What word can we use to express ourselves instead of using "stupid" to show how we feel?

Words have power even when we don't realize that we are using to break ourselves down and those around us.

CHAPTER 3

SELFISH

"You're so selfish to only think of yourself, what about me?"

Have you ever been in a relationship (boyfriend, girlfriend, even just friendships) where someone in your life may not understand or be open-minded to the things you do and your purpose for wanting to better yourself?

Having dreams and goals is not being selfish but putting yourself before others so it is going to help you become the person you want to be. Those that are in your life should be people who motivate you, push you, and want the best for you. If you are seeing that your circle of friends is a weight holding you down, then ask yourself these questions.

*Do they support my dreams and goals?

*How is my relationship with this person(s)?

*Do they genuinely care about me, or is this relationship/friendship becoming toxic?

If the answers to your questions are not matching to what you expected them to be, it is time to evaluate the people around you. Are these the same people who challenge your ideas/thoughts by saying, "that's dumb" or "don't be so stupid"?

Think about that.

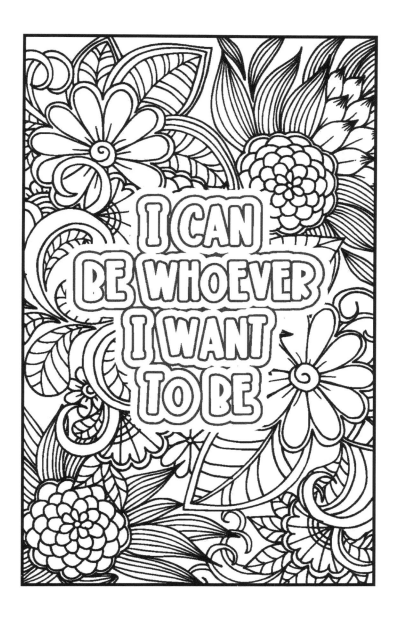

CHAPTER 4

CRAZY

Now this word… Drove me, CRAZY!

A person in my life for several years called me CRAZY all of the time, and it honestly became my 2nd name.

Everything I said, everything I did, every thought that ran through my mind was associated with being told, "you're crazy." I let this word take over my life even as a successful, educated, kind person I knew I was.

The word held so much power over me I lost myself and forgot who I was and I let it bring me down. It took having to learn how to love myself and remove myself from the negative word and environment to realize that what I wanted to do and become was CRAZY *AWESOME*!

See what I did there

At that moment, I decided that I wouldn't let the word crazy be a negative aspect of my life but use the word to MAKE my dreams and goals a reality!

Let's dive into this word and understand what it means to be CRAZY *(in a good way)* and jot down your answer on the Notes Section:

*What are 3 CRAZY things you have done for yourself?

*What would be a CRAZY Dream you feel can't be accomplished? (change that mindset and do it!)

*Instead of the word CRAZY what would you call it?

CHAPTER 5

ENOUGH

"You're just not good enough"

"You're not popular enough"

"You're not smart enough"

"You're not pretty enough"

"You're not tall enough"

"You don't write good enough"

"You don't have enough skills"

Do you know what I have to say about someone telling me what is enough?

ENOUGH IS *ENOUGH!* And it is time for a **CHANGE!**

Being enough for someone can mean something entirely different to another person. I want you to remember that someone's definition of enough is their own and only theirs. This BROKEN word does not define what you can learn, what you can become and what you can do.

Let's rewind ... remember when I told you my story about my teacher who told me I was not smart enough to be in their class. If you would of told me that at 14 years old I would be standing in front of that teacher and said, "Hey, don't worry, you're going to do great things!" I probably would have laughed and said yea right.

If you are going through this in your life right now, I want to tell you to not let a BROKEN word such as ENOUGH take power over you, let it be a word that will push you towards success!

CHAPTER 6

USELESS

"Who are you to tell me that I am less than what I should be..."

– BarlowGirls

When I entered high school, I was introduced to this girl band named Barlow Girls and I noticed I always gravitated to this song called "Mirror."

The song talked about looking In the mirror and seeing yourself as someone that looked at themselves and felt they did not measure up to others' expectations.

If you feel that your parents, friends, teachers, or even yourself have high expectations and don't feel like you could ever measure up because you feel useless, I want you to change that mindset today.

I want you to list the expectations for yourself and what others may have for you.

Now, take a second look at your list, are you comfortable with those expectations? Do they push you for success? Or does it set you up for failure? Do you feel useless just looking at the long list of high expectations from others or yourself?

After this exercise, I want you to go to a mirror and look at yourself and repeat these words:

"Who are you to tell me that I am less than what I should be."

"You don't define me."

The person looking back at you in the mirror was your old self, your new self knows you are NOT USELESS! You are special and can accomplish any expectations you set your mind to.

CHAPTER 7

WEAK

Just saying the word weighs heavy on the heart, on the mind and the body!

What does it mean to be weak?

Is it physical?

Is it mental?

Is it environmental?

Let's, look at each one individually to see where we feel we might be weak and find the strength to overcome these challenges.

Physical weakness

I remember the day I was standing in the center of the football field during half-time under bright lights and hearing the people on the stands cheering. I was in the dance team and getting ready to do our Friday night performance when I broke down and found myself on the floor with a knee that was no longer functioning. I eventually had to get surgery and was told I was no longer needed on the team. It was that day I found myself physically weak and not wanting to get up and continue going.

If you felt physically weak, how can you find strength at that moment?

Mental Weakness

WORDS have POWER and I've talked to you about the many words that can break down our self-esteem, our self-worth and our mindset. If any word on this list has brought back a memory of a time when it made you feel mentally weak, I want you to let that be in the past and think of positive words we will talk about later on in the book. If there has been a BROKEN word lingering in your mind since you started this book, I want you to write it down in a piece of paper and hold on to it until you finish reading this book *(we will come back to this word later.)* Remember, you hold power to these words, and you will not let it become your weakness.

Environmental Weakness

Ever been around a group of friends who just seem to give up at the sight of a challenge? Do you come from a home where family members tell you you can't go to college because no one in the family has? Or have you ever noticed that the people around you seem to speak negatively?

"Monkey see, monkey do" have you heard that phrase?

When we are surrounded by this environment, we fall into those habits as well and don't realize that we have become followers of those who don't want to succeed.

Which of the following three have you found yourself under?

How can we overcome these weaknesses and find the strength to do what we want to do.

CHAPTER 8

CAN'T

"You can't move far away"

"You can't go to college"

"You can't get that job"

"You can't get anybody to love you"

I want to share this incredible story with you about someone told they simply can do none of the above. I was sitting down at a conference one day listening to one motivational speaker and he talked about some very pivotal moments in his life.

His mother was in and out of prison, moved from city to city, and flipped between schools. His family told him, "You can't go to college" because, no one in his family had ever been. His school counselor told him, "You can't move far away" because no one in his small-town school had ever moved away to a big prestigious university. He eventually became a top honor graduate from his high school and moved to Washington DC, where he attended the prestigious Georgetown University where many US

Presidents send their kids! Talk about turning CAN'T to I CAN!

When someone says you CAN'T, it is because their thinking is limited and not open to learning more, this is where you come in and say I CAN.

What is something you have always wanted to accomplish but have been told you can't?

(Write it down, statistics show that if you write something down, you are 42% more likely to achieve it!)

CHAPTER 9

WEIRD

Is being weird all that bad? Last time I checked, that just meant I was one of a kind and special.

When you associate the phrase "dude, you are weird," it makes us feel isolated and wanting to hide away because we aren't seen as anybody else. But who is to say that being like everyone else is just too ordinary?

When did it ever become WEIRD to be unique, to be special, to be a one of a kind person?

Think of this way.

If a group of people at school or outside of school say, "you're such a weirdo," take a deep look and who they are and who they are hanging around with. Often you will see there is one leader in the group and the rest are followers. You, however, stand out and have a unique personality and quality to you they feel should not be broadcasted to the world, so they make you feel less than.

So, the next time someone calls you weird just say, "Yea I know I'm unique."

If you change the narrative, they will change their
perspective!

CHAPTER 10

NO

"I want to join the team" *NO!*

"I want to take this class" *NO!*

"I want to move to the big city for college" *NO!*

"I want to have a career in _____" *NO!*

I guess you can say NO is a lot like CAN'T, but in this case, it cuts in a little deeper because not

only does the person not think you are capable, now the person telling you NO does not BELIEVE in you and does NOT want you to do it!

I come from a small town deep down in south Texas, literally right at the border of Mexico and something we see so often is Hispanic parents telling their kids NO! Our generation is changing rapidly with the goals of moving to the big city, going to college, and getting our dream job. But, our parents sometimes have the mentality you are leaving the family and not wanting to help in the household.

If you come from a home you feel does not understand what you want to do in your life ok, they might not understand because they grew up in a generation where those dreams were not attainable and have to survive in the best way they knew how.

Even at school, having friends or teachers/coaches tell you NO doesn't mean you are not capable. They just haven't had the chance to see your talents. The next time someone tells you NO, respond with watch me! Change the BROKEN words into a POWERFUL positive word! It is all on how you change that mindset!

CHAPTER 11

BORING

"OMG you're so boring"

Have your friends ever told you that before?

Mine have, often !

So I didn't want to go to that party?

So I didn't want to drink alcohol?

So I didn't want to "do it"?

So I didn't want to do drugs?

What is the definition of boring?

A person who does not want to do something that makes them uncomfortable or knows that it is wrong.

As far as I know, I was true and that is all that mattered. I did not tell myself that during those moments, I was called BORING by friends, but I later realized that I was not a follower but just being my own person.

Being boring doesn't mean I don't like fun or participate in social gatherings. I just knew when the right time and place.

Just because someone calls your BORING doesn't mean you are. That person just doesn't like for others to go against what they are doing because they want to feel that what they are doing is ok. So don't feel bad telling someone no or that you don't want to when you know, it isn't right.

CHAPTER 12

DISAPPOINTMENT

Have you ever felt disappointed by something?

Maybe you did not get the grade you expected in class?

Maybe someone you liked did not feel the same way about you?

Maybe a friend let you down?

Or

Your teacher said, "You disappointed me"

Your parents said, "You're such a disappointment"

Your friends tell you, "Don't disappointment this weekend!"

How does that make you feel?

Nervous

Sad

Regret

Angry

Disappointment is "sadness or displeasure caused by the nonfulfillment of one's hopes or expectations."

Even though the word disappointment can be crushing, let it be a motivator.

How? You may ask.

If you think back to what made that person feel you were a disappointment, I want you to use that moment for growth and motivation.

For example:

You did not make the varsity team and you felt disappointed in yourself and you go home and tell your parents and they say, "Well, that is just disappointing."

Instead of letting that get you down and keep you down, think of a way to help you get motivated.

-Practice more in and out of school

-Ask the coach what you need more work on and sharpen that skill

-Try again!

As Martin Luther King Jr said, "We must accept finite disappointment, but never lose infinite hope."

Remember, there will always be a disappointment, not everyone will have your best interest at heart and not everyone will help you succeed. Don't lose hope on what you want to accomplish and work hard for what you want, not what others want for you.

CHAPTER 13

FAILURE

According to Webster's dictionary online, failure is defined as:

omission of occurrence or performance

specifically: a <u>failing</u> to perform a duty or expected action

Did you catch the word *expected action?*

Our parents have high expectations for us and rightfully so they want us to do better and to work hard. However, the reality is that we might not meet all of their expectations to their standards.

So we tell ourselves, "I am such a failure."

From 6th grade, until I graduated high school, I was always involved in sports and especially track & field.

I remember after every track meet when my dad would pick me up the first question he would ask me was, "So, what place did you get?"

I was not the fastest runner, but I also wasn't the slowest, I was an average athlete that sometimes got 4th or other times I got 2nd.

This is how most of our car ride conversations went:

Dad: So, what place did you get?

Me: Oh, I got 3rd place!!

Dad: Well, you should have gotten 1st!

Even in academics, I was set to a high standard, especially during report card time. Conversations at home went just about the same way with my extra-curricular activities:

Me: Hey, dad, I got my report card! I passed!

Dad: What were your grades?

Me: Well I got a 90, 80, and 86

Dad: You should have gotten a 100, 90, and 96!

With each conversation I felt like I failed. I did not meet my dad's standards. But, I realized that not that I was a failure in his eyes or that I wasn't good enough or smart enough. My dad just wanted to push me to my fullest potential, and it was something I learned as I got much older.

So, if there is anything to take away from this is to realize that you are not a FAILURE! If you have people around you pushing you and have high expectations, it is because they care.

"I can accept failure, everyone fails at something. But I can't accept not trying." – Michael Jordan

CHAPTER 14

WRONG

You raise your hand in class to share your thoughts and answer the question being asked.

"WRONG"

What a defeating word to be told in front of others, isn't it?

Your forehead between your eyebrows scrunch up, face looking confused on why or how am I wrong?

You want to reach for the stars and have big dreams and aspirations. You share them with friends and family and they say that's WRONG! That's not for you!

That hit right in the heart, didn't it?

Often people don't understand how to respond to someone's ideas and so when they come back with WRONG, it cuts deep.

Instead of telling someone they are wrong they should respond with "Not the best answer, but let's dig in more to find out what the answer maybe" or "I don't think that is right in my opinion, but share with me a little more on your thoughts."

Did that have a different feeling?

Remember, not all of your friends and family will agree with your ideas. That doesn't mean they are wrong or that you are wrong. It just means that person and yourself have a different viewpoint on things. So, the next time someone responds to you with the word WRONG, reflect to what I just said and remember they just have a different idea of what is right and what is wrong.

CHAPTER 15

IN THE WAY

I step to the side, and I try to make myself not be so visible because I've been told, "You're just in the way."

Feeling like you don't belong or have the feeling of being a nuisance to someone can be lonely.

This is a common feeling, and I hope you never have to experience it, but if you're like most teens you probably have had someone tell you that or maybe you have told a friend those same words do not realize the effect it might have on them.

If it is one thing you take away from the 15 BROKEN word list we just went through is that you are never in someone's way. Every person has their destiny and road to follow, and if they allow someone to stand in their way, it is just an excuse for them to go down a different path.

A person who says the words "You are in the way" are people who want to make you feel insignificant and useless. Now go back a few pages and re-read what it means to be useless and look at yourself in the mirror again and say, "Who are you to tell me what I should be."

No one should ever have the POWER to hold BROKEN words over you.

Let's break down the BROKEN words we just discussed and let's replace those words with the positive POWER words. Remember, you cannot always control what other people say or what comes out of their mouths, but you can control how you take those words in. Words are Power, and only you can control the power the words will have in your life.

"Throughout human history, our greatest leaders and thinkers have used the power of words to transform our emotions, to enlist us in their causes, and to shape the course of destiny. Words can not only create emotions. They create actions. And from our actions flow the results of our lives."

Tony Robbins

YOUR WORDS HAVE POWER. USE THEM WISELY.

CHAPTER 16

SMART

Did you know that I didn't hear the word SMART being said to me until I was in my 20s? Crazy, isn't it?

The power of being called smart uplifts your self-esteem, but it should also be something you tell yourself daily.

Now, we might not be experts in every subject, but we have to find our strength in what we feel comfortable with and make it your expertise.

Remember, broken word #1 Dumb that is not you. You are smart in so many ways. You just have to tap into your expertise.

List 3 things you feel you are smart at?

1. _____

2. _____

3. _____

For example,

I am very bad in math, does that make me not smart? Not necessarily, I am very strong in reading and writing and so I feel I am smart in those areas.

So if you haven't been told yet that you are smart like I hadn't until I was in my mid-20s don't feel you aren't. You just need to look back at the list you wrote above.

CHAPTER 17

PASSIONATE

Going back to that time, I was called "Crazy" I realized that the things I was crazy about were actually just my passion for what I wanted to do in my life.

If you want to be the next president or become the next NBA basketball player, then do everything in your power to make sure you achieve those dreams.

As long as it is a passion, then you are set for success.

Don't let anyone deter you away from your passion or make you feel you are crazy for having those dreams. Share your passion with others and you will be surprised who will be with you every step of the way. Those actions are powerful in that the people surrounded by you will see the passion you have and it will empower others to do the same.

Here is a checklist and questions to go through to make sure your passion keeps on burning!

1. What drives you and motivates you to follow your passions?

2. Who pushes you to continue working on what you are most passionate about?

3. What are you doing today to make sure that what you are passionate about is achieved?

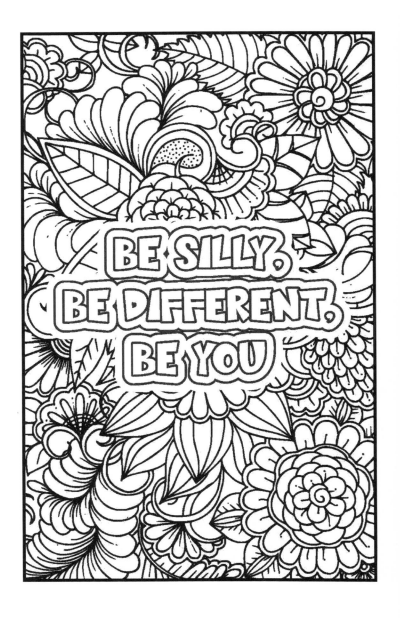

CHAPTER 18

VALUABLE

What does it mean to be valuable?

1 adj If you describe something or someone as **valuable***, you mean that they are very useful and helpful.*

Every person in this world has value. Your life has value; your purpose in this world has value.

Whenever you feel you are not of value to others, they might not see what you have to offer. But, don't let that distract you from the fact that you were born to have a purpose and whatever that may be, it will be valuable to the right person.

Imagine being told by your teacher, future boss, a college professor you have brought VALUE into the classroom/company/college.

Wouldn't that feel great?

So as you figure out your passion as we talked about earlier, use that to bring value into other people's lives. You never know who you will come across that will find your uniqueness and passions valuable.

CHAPTER 19

CAPABLE

To that person that has ever told you you CAN'T or just straight up shot you down and said NO.

Well, I have this to say, I can do anything I set my mind to and I hope that as we have been going through our POWER words you feel the same way.

Let me share with you a story about a time I was told I CAN'T.

Throughout high school I was very involved in dance, cheer, and sports! Especially track and field. My freshman year was probably my best year yet, making the JV Cheer Team and making VARSITY in track and field.

It was during my sophomore year that things started falling apart, at least in my eyes my life was crumbling over. It was the year I decided I also wanted to be part of the competitive dance team and was getting ready to go to our first competition the day after our 1st track meet of the season. As I was getting ready at the starting line, feet on the blocks waiting for the gun to go off in the back of my mind I was also very excited for the next day!

Jumping hurdle after hurdle getting close to the finish line, I never made it. Next thing I know I am on the side of the track on the floor with the athletic trainer, my coach, and other athletes hovering over me. I had just torn ligaments in my knee, my trip to the dance competition was over, my track season was over.

The doctors and athletic trainer informed me that I would be out for the next year and couldn't participate in athletics. This moment was a hard blow, especially right in the middle of my high school athletic career.

I was told you can't, but I knew that if I worked hard with my physical therapy and trained properly I could get back to what I love. It only took me a few months before I was back on the track running and back on the football field dancing during the half time shows.

So what is my take away from this experience that I want you to take and run with?

There might be moments that will knock you down, those who think this is it! It's over, you can't.

Well, you are capable of doing whatever you set your mind to if you really want it.

1. What are you capable of doing?

2. How will you show others that you are capable?

3. What will you tell those people that say you can't?

"Put all excuses aside and remember this: YOU are capable." – Zig Ziglar

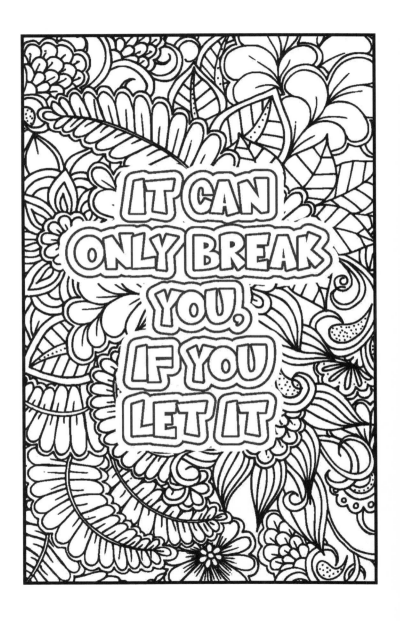

CHAPTER 20

IMPORTANT

Have you seen the movie *The Help* in that powerful scene when the character says, "You is smart. You is Kind. You is IMPORTANT."

You have the power every day to show others how important they are, and you have the power to remind yourself that in this world you are important to your family, to your friends, and your teachers. You might not feel it every day, you might not hear it every day, but remember that you are an important person to someone.

I will never forget the day when I was entering 7th grade and my mom got a call that one of my good friends had gone missing, I was asked if I had seen her or heard from her, but I hadn't. Back in those days, we didn't have cell phones to text each other and see if we were ok. My friend came from a bad home and she was someone most moms would probably say don't be hanging around troubled girls like that, but we were friends. I remember arriving at school and heading to my first class of the day, and I couldn't stop thinking about my missing friend when suddenly, she popped up in the hallway as if nothing had happened. She told me she came to school because she knew I would be there and at that moment, I realized that I was important to someone and had made change in her life.

So, when doubting yourself if whether or not your life is important or has meaning, don't underestimate looking up to you.

CHAPTER 21

INFLUENTIAL

To be influential is to have a great influence on someone or something.

This is a 2 part story of how someone influenced my life in a great way and how I returned that appreciation in a time of my life I will never forget.

Part 1

I was going into my 10th-grade year of high school and one of my neighborhood best friends was finally coming to high school with me as an incoming freshman. Now, I had never ridden the bus in the morning to school because I had the luxury of going to school with my dad since he was a high school teacher (yay! Did you catch my sarcasm lol)?

My friend Lisa had always gone on the bus to and from school because you see she didn't come from a family with many luxuries, like many of us she struggled, but we helped each other through some good and bad times. Till this day I don't think she's ever known, not even to this day how influential she was on my life. She taught me the basics of cooking, cleaning, and how to do laundry the correct way (don't mix colors with white unless you want funky looking clothes).

You see, she had greater responsibilities than most teenagers I knew. Her older siblings worked late and hard to provide for the household and her mom was legally blind. Her job was to take care of the many tasks our mothers do for us such as cooking, cleaning, doing laundry and taking care of the household overall, so her mother really relied on her help at home. As I saw her help her mom and her family, she touched my life in a way that I will forever cherish and has been of great influence in my life today.

So ask yourself:

Who has been the most influential person in your life?

How can you be a great influence to others?

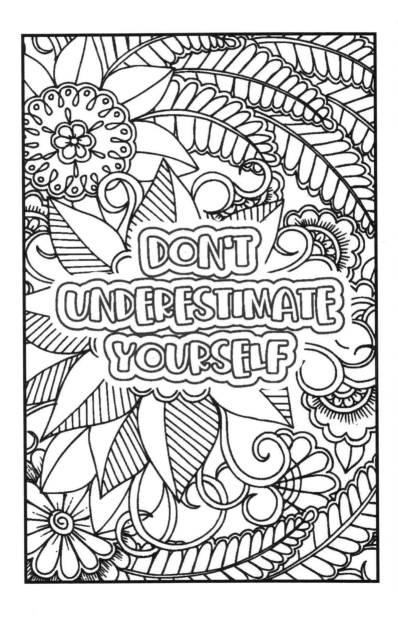

CHAPTER 22

APPRECIATED

Part 2

It was the night before going back to school, with teen girl excitement. I called up my friend Lisa to see what time I should meet her in the morning to go on the bus together. The voice on the other end of the phone didn't sound as excited as mine. She tells me they couldn't afford school supplies this year, or shoes, or the school's mandatory uniform. That moment broke me, but I remembered that all this time, she has helped me grow and taught me the simplest things in life. I knew that I had to do something.

I remember running to my parent's room and pleading to my mom we had to do something! Without hesitation, my mom and I quickly went to my friend Lisa's house and picked her and her little brother up and headed to the nearest Wal-Mart to get some school supplies and a few clothes to start them for school.

Till this day, she thanks our family and appreciates that time when we helped them. Now, I am not sharing this story to gloat on how we helped a family, but how I learned to appreciate everyone around me. I learned a great lesson at the age of 14 that we must always appreciate the simplest things in life. I learned that we help others just because we can. I appreciated my mom more than ever at that moment because she knew what was important to me and helping a family that had taught me so much about appreciating the smallest things in life.

Who do you appreciate most in life?

I want you to think deep and hard on that question and when you find your answer, I want you to contact that person and tell them to thank you!

It is a POWERFUL feeling of feeling appreciated but even more POWERFUL when you tell those important people in your life how much you appreciate them.

CHAPTER 23

COMMITTED

What does it mean to committed? Feeling dedication and loyalty to a cause, activity, or job;

Wholeheartedly dedicated.

The world will try to tell you that leaders are born and that it takes someone special to stay committed. The world will try to tell you you just have "it" or you do not have "it." Perhaps some of us are born with "it." What is "it?" Perhaps they mean some special commitment gene. Perhaps they mean some gift. Perhaps they mean something unexplainable. Whatever the "it" is, I did not have "it" when I committed to passing all of my classes, I did not have "it" when I left the team, and I did not have "it" when I stopped going to graduate school.

Can you relate to feeling like you don't have "it?" or do you feel like you have "it" already?

Whether you feel you have "it" or not, you need to commit to what you have signed yourself up. You need to commit to yourself not to give up when things get hard.

I remember feeling very *disappointed* when I stopped going to school, where I was working on my Ph.D. because it was a life goal I had set for myself since I was 15. I remember feeling *discouraged* when I kept making the B's and Cs in my classes. I remember feeling *deflated* when I thought I was good at Cheer but again made the JV team or always making the C team in volleyball and basketball.

I watched as other classmates were having success in the classroom. I watched as other students would have success as an individual. I watched as the athletes make the "better" team.

What I watched most was that the best students and athletes committed to being the best versions of themselves. The best student committed to succeeding. The best student committed even when the teacher, other students, and coaches were not looking. The successful student were committed.

As I watched others succeed, I learned the meaning of commitment, so if you are feeling discouraged or deflated as I did, then pick yourself up and become committed to at least one thing you find to be your biggest passion. Staying committed may not happen overnight, but it's taking a start is all that matters.

It's not where you start, but where you finish. You just have to COMMIT.

CHAPTER 24

FOCUSED

Have you ever had friends tell you that you no longer have time for them?

They might say "you think you are too good for us now?"

Or maybe they feel that you being focused on your dreams and goals is being SELFISH.

Whatever other people may think of you, there is nothing wrong in FOCUSING on yourself! Remember you hold the power to your life and the direction you decide to take is all up to you, not others.

If you find yourself having friends who are holding you back from what you want to do and focus on take another look at the circle of people that are around you.

Always surround yourself with like-minded group of people who will understand what you want to do and why you want to do it.

Having a support system to back you up while you are focusing on what you want to do will only help you become successful and achieve all that you want to do.

There was a time in my life when I was really focusing on my career and school goals, I had always told myself I want to achieve the greatest degree there is to offer, a PhD. It was during that time when I found myself applying and getting accepted into the doctoral program at Our Lady of the Lake University, a highly acclaimed private university in Texas. I was focused and ready to take on this challenge for the next four years and I knew that having my support system would only give me the push I needed to make sure I stayed on track and focused. However, that excitement and hope of encouragement quickly faded when the person I was dating at the time quickly shot me down by making fun of my achievements and making it known that no matter what degree I had or accolades I attained I would never measure up to him, I was still not good enough or smart enough.

It was right there and then that I knew if I wanted to focus on me, I had to let that person go immediately.

Ask yourself the following questions:

- Look into your life, who is around you?

- Is there a person(s) that you need to let go of?

- Who is your biggest supporter and who is not?

CHAPTER 25

UNIQUE

Do you find yourself being different than others? Do you notice you don't keep friendships for long? Or do you see you like to go against the norm?

I have found that I've had people tell me, "You're weird," "why are you doing that?" or "no one does that." Doing things differently doesn't mean I shouldn't do it or that I am weird, but rather I have a UNIQUE way of thinking and a UNIQUE personality.

So what does it mean to be UNIQUE? Why is being UNIQUE powerful?

- Being unique means you don't follow anyone.

- Being unique means having the freedom to do whatever your heart desires.

- Being unique means going against the grain and not following the "norm".

- Being unique means starting your own trends.

- Being unique means, you will come across many people during every different part of your life's journey. I can't say I have the same friends from elementary, middle school, high school, not even college today! As I change through my stages in life, I meet people and create friendships on the same path as me. That is the power of freedom and being unique and different.

- Being unique means taking ownership of it, having pride in that uniqueness.

- Being unique means taking on new challenges that others might not take on due to fear of change and the unknown.

- Be brave, follow your uniqueness and differences.

Ask yourself what makes you different? What makes you unique?

Quotes to Remember:

"Why fit in, when you were born to stand out"

– Dr. Seuss

"In order to be irreplaceable one must always be different" – Coco Chanel

"You have to be unique, and different, and shine in your own way" – Lady Gaga

CHAPTER 26

WORTHY

As I was researching for what it meant to be worthy, I came across several types of definitions I didn't agree with.

One definition said, "To be worthy is to be entitled to respect and attention."

Another said, "You are worthy because of accomplishments and awards you are qualified to receive."

Did you notice how these definitions of being considered worthy were by getting the acceptance or recognition of being worthy by someone else?

Who gets to decide whether you are WORTH IT?

Why do other people get to decide if you are WORTH IT?

We've learned that people's words are powerful and can be used against us to make us believe that we are not worthy of being accepted, loved, or appreciated. So, when we hear the BROKEN words we discussed earlier repeatedly we tell ourselves that we are not WORTHY.

We believe what we are told rather than changing our mindset to believe otherwise.

Because let me tell you something,

YOU ARE WORTHY! YOU ARE ACCEPTED! YOU ARE LOVED! YOU ARE APPRECIATED!

So let's create our own definition of WORTHY!

Synonyms: Valuable, honest, helpful, importance

Definition: To be Worthy is to be valuable, to be honest, and helpful and

someone who is important.

Who gets to decide now who is WORTHY? Only You!

CHAPTER 27

FIERCE

Have you ever checked your zodiac sign and tried to compare personality and character traits to see if you matched?

I am a LEO and according to my horoscope, I should be a person that is intelligent, warm, and courageous. The fire sign of Leo is characterized as someone who is a natural leader and someone that makes a name for themselves.

That is one very BOLD characteristic of a person that is born a LEO.

Is this really me? Well, I will be honest that every time I read my horoscope through high school, I always laughed and said yup that is NOT ME at all! I am shy, quiet, not a leader, and not someone trying to make a name for themselves.

For as long as I can remember, I have always had a fear of change or doing something different than my peers because I felt I would fail or be judged for trying something new that I could embarrass myself doing.

But I've learned through life that being FIERCE and taking challenges head-on have made the person I am today, and I feel that I have made a name for myself.

I think we can all be our true authentic selves. We just haven't dug deep to find that FIERCE personality we all have built-in ourselves.

Taking on leadership roles was not something I ever saw myself doing or having the courage to speak in front of adult people (I say this because I was a teacher and speaking in front of a classroom and front of a room full of adults is different!).

So what does it mean to be FIERCE? It means that when the going gets tough, you can stand tall and push through it! It means being ferocious and forceful, like a lion. It means being strong and proud, dangerous, and ready to take on anything you set your mind to!

That is the power of being FIERCE!

CHAPTER 28

UNLIMITED

The only limits that exist are the ones in your own mind." Anonymous.

Have you ever set a goal for yourself but stopped yourself short?

Do you have dreams and think to yourself there is no way I can do that?

What are you afraid of?

Why are you setting limits to what you can do?

So many questions and so many ways to knock those doubts down and give yourself NO LIMITS!

When you want to do something so bad, I want you to write this down anywhere near you right now!

You have NO LIMITS

You can ACHIEVE IT

You can DREAM IT

You can DO IT

Now really repeat that to yourself OVER and OVER until you BELIEVE IT!

There are no limits to what you can do, and that is a great POWER to have because only you can go beyond it or stay behind that line of limitation.

Don't let others hold that power over you when you have dreams and aspirations and people tell you it is impossible or that all you can do is so much (that is putting a line down and limiting your capabilities.)

CROSS THAT LINE into pushing the limits!

How will you CROSS THAT LINE?

How will you go BEYOND YOUR LIMITS?

CHAPTER 29

RESILIENCE

A POWERFUL word I want you to take hold of is
Resilience.

What does that mean exactly?

A person who is resilient means you are strong in the face
of adversity, you let go of things that don't matter and you
allow no one to tell you that you can't.

You are the person determined and committed.

You are the person with courage and curiosity.

You are the person that motivates yourself and faces
challenges head-on.

You are the person caring and accepts support from
others.

We've talked about how words can make or break you
mentally, emotionally, and physically and how changing
those words into positivity and using the power of words
to build ourselves up is being this – RESELIENT!

Mental Resilience is taking on challenges that may seem difficult, but you fight through and motivate yourself to accomplish anything you set your MIND to,

Emotional Resilience is changing the BROKEN power word and find the POSITIVE in it! Remember when we talked about people saying you can't and digging dig and telling yourself yes I CAN! Only you have the power to let go of the negative and bring in the positive.

Physical Resilience is being there for someone and encourage those around you. Remember that you attract what you put out. Be that person that provides support and you will see how others will do the same for you. Always surround yourself with people who will be there for you to help you and push you when times get tough.

CHAPTER 30

EMPOWERING

I want you to answer these questions of what we have learned so far:

Have you learned how to take the POWER OF WORDS and take charge of them?

YES OR NO

Have you learned not to let others have POWER over you with BROKEN WORDS?

YES OR NO

Have you learned to take BROKEN WORDS into POWERFUL WORDS?

YES OR NO

Now I hope you have been able to answer YES to the questions I just asked. I want you to take what you have learned and teach your friends, family, and anyone else around you how the POWER OF WORDS can make or break your self-esteem, mindset, and Self-Worth. I want you to be that person who EMPOWERS others to continue being their best versions of themselves.

Remember, you have the POWER now and use it to help others learn how to use their WORDS.

Empower doesn't always mean to give someone else the power or authority, but in this case, we are passing the torch. We are passing the power to understand how we are worthy, we are important, we are intelligent and we are influential!

"What you love, you empower. What you fear, you empower. What you empower, you attract."

- Anonymous

FINAL THOUGHTS

I hope that as you went through the 30 POWERFUL and BROKEN words and that you have learned how to turn a negative situation into a powerful positive outcome.

REMEMBER

YOU hold the POWER to change your mindset, YOU have the POWER to push away the words that break down our SELF-ESTEEM, because only YOU have the POWER to know what you are WORTH! And trust me your SELF-WORTH is important.

NEVER FORGET

1. Just as you have learned about the power of words, teach those around you as well.

   "Be careful with your words, once they are said, they can be only forgiven, not forgotten."

   – Anonymous

2. People will tell you that you can't. Doesn't mean they are right.

   "The ones who say you can't are too afraid you will."

   – Nike

3. There will be times that you will doubt yourself, don't let it over power you.

   "Success at anything will always come down to this: Focus and effort, and we control both."

   – Dwayne "The Rock" Johnson

4. Find a person that influences you in a great way and build on those relationships.

   "The people you surround yourself with influence your behaviors, so choose friends who have healthy habits."

   – Dan Buettner

5. Don't let anyone make you feel that you are not good enough or not smart enough. You are enough!

   "I am Enough, I have always been enough, I will always be enough." - Anonymous

10 DAY CHALLENGE

Day 1:

Post your POWER WORD on any social media platform.

#powerofwords

Day 2:

Text 1 Friend: "Hey you should know you are

_____."

Choose any power word from the book or your own.

Day 3:

Call (not text) 1 Friend who feels broken: "Hey you should know you are _____."

Choose any power word of encouragement from the book or your own.

Day 4:

Take a selfie with a piece of paper written with a POWER Word and post on a social media platform.

#powerofwords

Day 5:

On a Post it Note, write down a POWER Word and stick it to your mirror and read it to yourself every morning.

Day 6:

Text 2 Friends: "You are _____." And tell them to text 2 other friends. Let the chain of power of positivity continue!

Day 7:

Share your favorite chapter with 3 friends.

Day 8:

Take a selfie with a group of friends, each one with a sheet of paper sharing their POWER Word. Post it on any social media platform.

#powerofwords

Day 9:

Call (no texting) 2 Friends and share a time you overcame a challenge.

Day 10:

Write down a BROKEN WORD that is still in your heart, TEAR IT! BURN IT! Or TOSS IT! And LEAVE IT BEHIND!

ACKNOWLEDGMENTS

There are so many people that I want to dedicate this book to, but I really want to thank my amazing partner Jonathan Medina for being by my side every step of the way while writing this book. It was a time where we went deep into our past and helped each other grow to understand what it means to empower one another. For inspiring me and motivating me as well as pushing me to step out of my comfort and share my story with you the readers.

A big thank you to my wonderful sisters in Christ, Daisy, Mariel, Judith, Lizzy, Katherine, Jennifer, Amalia, and Victoria. You girls have helped me become the strong woman I am today, you have taught me to give, to love, and flourish and for that I am blessed beyond measure to have had you by my side as my personal cheerleaders. I love you ladies.

To a leader who has inspired me to dream big, achieve big, and push passed the horizon, Ms. Marina Abdullah. You are the symbol for woman empowerment and I am so honored and blessed that I was able to work and learn from you these past few years. You will forever be engraved in my heart and I thank you for always telling me to just DO IT! Fear was never in your vocabulary and that is something I will hold dear forever.

Lastly, to my family, Mom, Dad and Michael. You all have taught me from a young age that if I want to accomplish my dreams and goals I just had to go for it. You've watched me struggle and rise through the challenges but you helped me become the strong, smart and independent woman I am today.

I love you all.

Notes

_____

_____

_____

_____

_____

_____

_____

_____

_____

_____

_____

_____

_____

Notes

_____

_____

_____

_____

_____

_____

_____

_____

_____

_____

_____

_____

_____

_____

_____

Notes

Notes

_____

_____

_____

_____

_____

_____

_____

_____

_____

_____

_____

_____

_____

_____

Made in the USA
Middletown, DE
05 May 2022